Cincinnati & Soup

A Second Helping

More Recipes from the Queen City

by Cheri Brinkman

ISBN-10: 0-615-49318-1
ISBN-13: 978-0-6154-9318-3

First Edition 2011

Mac Guffin Productions
cincinnatiandsoup@yahoo.com
www.VintageCincinnati.Etsy.com

Cover & Design:
Erin Beckloff :: iNkY WiNKe
inkywinky.etsy.com

Postcard (Cover Art):
Roebling Bridge & Skyline from Ohio River, Cincinnati
Kraemer Art. Co. Cincinnati, Ohio circa 1925

Undated Newspaper Clippings: The Cincinnati Enquirer,
The Cincinnati Post and The Times Star

This book is dedicated to my dear
(and long suffering) husband Ed and
my daughter Allison without whose
good humor, eating and encouragement
this would not have been possible.

After the great success of my first book: *Cincinnati & Soup: Recipes from the Queen City & Great Soup*, I initially wanted to work on a Cincinnati Festival Book which I have been researching. In the meantime I have gotten countless emails and "tips" about other old recipes and of course more great Cincinnati nostalgia to send along to you who are still longing for tearooms, white gloves and a bit more civility in real life.

This book has MORE of what you really enjoy– Cincinnati nostalgia, as well as more recipes from the great old days. So get ready for more great recipes from Shillito's, Wray Jean Braun (Mrs. Bob Braun), Colleen Sharp, The 50-50 Club to name drop–recipes which jump the Ohio from our neighbors in Covington and Newport and, of course, some more new soups.

The Cincinnati cooking adventure continues with
a 2nd helping...Yes sir – I want some more!!!

Cheri Brinkman
2011

Table of Contents

Table of Contents CONTINUED

Cincinnati Nostalgia

Turn on those old black and white sets and adjust those rabbit ears – we are tuning in to our classic Cincinnati radio and television friends. Swing by Fountain Square enroute to more adventures downtown...

Everybody's Farm

Perhaps you were one of the lucky Cincinnati grade schoolers who at least once in their school career were carted off to WLW's country studio for a day at the "farm"? This farm was located on a long bus ride out Highway 42 in the real "country" north of Mason, Ohio. You had to bring a brown bag lunch for the long trip.

Everybody's Farm began in 1941 and was a real working farm located near the intersection of US 42 and the Snider Road Connector. From the 1940's through the 1960's this was one of Warren County's largest tourist attractions. Visitors were able to tour fields, barns and chicken coops- and they did by the thousands! A little white studio was built as a location for the station to actually broadcast from the farm.

Some of the more famous programs which WLW broadcast from the farm included:

Everybody's Farm: A noon radio program – which also included the farm reports from the futures markets in Chicago.

Chore Time: A morning radio program; broadcast from the barn or other farm sites.

Farm Front: A television program broadcast on Saturdays.

Everybody's Farm is gone and the property was recently on sale for over $1,000,000. What lives on are the great memories of those field trips and standing very very quiet while the announcer read the the noon market statistics... and of course seeing real cows and real chickens instead of being in a stuffy classroom!

I have yet to find a recipe from *Everybody's Farm* – so I am sharing with you my modern "quick" recipe for an old fashioned favorite: Chicken and Dumplings.

Chicken & Dumplings Revisited

Fresh from the Farm – so simple any "cluck" can make this!

CHICKEN STEW:

1 ½ cup cooked chicken
2 cans cream of chicken soup
1 cup chopped cooked carrots
1 cup thawed frozen peas
2 Tblsp dried minced onions
1 cup milk
½ cup white wine
1 Tblsp garlic powder
1 Tblsp dried parsley
*OPTIONAL: Add 8 fresh mushrooms sliced very thin.

1. Mix all of the above together.
   IF it looks too thick – add ⅓ cup of water.
2. Simmer and stir to a boil.

The best dumplings for this I have ever made are from a "baking mix" (i.e. something along the lines of Bisquick

DUMPLINGS:

1 cup baking mix
4 Tblsp water

1. Combine mix with water and make a dough.
   You don't want it too sticky, you want a dough.
2. Drop by spoonfuls into the steaming chicken stew.
3. Simmer together about 10 minutes.
   Then cover for 10 minutes and continue to simmer.

Serve in bowls with a nice green salad on the side.
This should give you four hearty servings.

Bob Braun
CINCINNATI'S MR. TELEVISION

When working on this book it is hard to not think of Ruth Lyons and the 50-50 Club without thinking of her co-host for years and then her successor, Bob Braun.

Bob had an absolutely amazing career in local broadcasting. From being a lifeguard at Coney Island, Bob parlayed into a singing career with his rich baritone voice , a recording artist and of course a local personality. He was a popular DJ with his Bob Braun's Bandstand in the 1960's on WLW radio and mc'd an afternoon movie as well as the Ruth Lyons show. On any given week he might be "on the air" 7 days a week with his radio and TV commitments.

Everyone in Cincinnati knew who Bob Braun was. He was a nice guy too. The first time I met Bob Braun was at the 50-50 Club after Ruth Lyons departed. My mother had written for tickets and they came after Ruth left the show. (The Ruth Lyons Show was so popular that you had to write in for tickets sometimes a year or two in advance!) We made our way to the studio in Crosley Square in downtown Cincinnati and up to the second floor where we sat on bleacher seats with a bunch of really dressed up women in hats and gloves to "wave" during the "hello" song. [CONTINUED]

It was a grand time for all. Music, exciting guests and food demonstrations, as well as prizes for the audience members who attended. People came from all over as the show was seen in not only Cincinnati, but Dayton, Columbus, Indianapolis Lexington and Huntington, to name a few places in the region.

I didn't see Bob again until after I had interned at WLW during my graduate school program. This was during the "last days" of the Bob Braun Show – which was what the 50-50 Club had become in the 1980's. I was looking for employment at the time and interviewed for a PR position on his staff. It wasn't to be, but I did finally get to meet Bob "in person." As it turned out the show wasn't on the air but two years more before it was cancelled and Bob went out West to follow other opportunities.

In the late 1990's I was lunching with some friends at the Montgomery Inn and ran into Bob over there. He was meeting some other people as well and gave his still sunny smile and happy wave. It seemed out of place to see him at lunch anywhere but on the 50-50 Club and on TV at noon.

The recipe I have is from Wray Jean Braun (Bob's wife) for her famous (and passed around a lot) Chicken and Noodles. I recently got to check that is was her recipe and yes – it is hers!

WRAY JEAN BRAUN'S

Chicken & Noodles

1 can of mushroom soup
6 chicken breasts
1 cup sour cream
12 oz noodles
salt and pepper to taste

DIRECTIONS:

1. Mix together the soup and sour cream. Spread half in a shallow baking pan.
2. Put salt and pepper on chicken breasts and place in the pan with the meat side up.
3. Top with the rest of the soup and sour cream.
4. Bake uncovered 1 ½ hours at 325°
5. During the last ½ hr. cook the noodles according to the package directions and drain. Stir into the chicken and sauce and serve.

Wray Jean suggests that she would use the boneless skinless chicken breasts when making this.

Ruth Lyons

50-50 CLUB COMMERCIAL FAVORITE

On of the great things about Ruth Lyons and the 50-50 Club were the commercials which she gave live during the program. She would write songs for the products as well as show actual recipes on the air using the sponsor's product.

There were tons of recipes given and often several times a week there would be one made up to see. These were popular recipes from the time and sometimes they would be repeated. Elsa Sule, who was one of Ruth's production team, sometimes created recipes with peanut butter. Ruth, of course, had a peanut butter sponsor. It is always a good footnote to these 50-50 Club recipes that Elsa, like Ruth, was an accomplished musician and not a professional chef, so the recipes given were usually really simple to do for Elsa and easy to give on the air for Ruth. The main supplier of the larger food items was Shillito's Dept. Store kitchens which made many of the dishes shown on the air. For a time during the Bob Braun years, Colleen Sharp did some of the culinary chores and later Beverly Nye, a local homemaker and author did the food "spots."

Remember the daytime audience was mainly homemakers at this time who with their little recipe file cards and trusty pencils had to be able to quickly write these down in a matter of minutes. Something too complicated would not work for these short spots. Of course you could always write the station for the recipe which was often done in those days too!

Peanut Butter Haystacks

1 cup butterscotch chips
½ cup peanut butter (smooth)
½ cup salted peanuts
2 cup chow mein noodles

DIRECTIONS:

1. Melt together the butterscotch chips and the peanut butter in a double boiler.
   (this is from the original instructions – today when you make these you can do this in the microwave in about 30-45 seconds)
2. Carefully stir in the peanuts and the noodles.
3. Drop by the spoonful onto wax paper.
4. Cool until set.

Colleen Sharp

"THE LORD WILL PROVIDE..."

At least that is what I remember her saying often on *The Paul Dixon Show* during the 1970's. Colleen was the cute and perky blonde singer on the Dixon show and later, after Paul's untimely death in 1974, joined the cast of the Bob Braun Show. Colleen, who was born in Indiana, always has had this amazing positive attitude and brought her Christian ideals to her television work. This wasn't surprising as Colleen was married to a pastor.

I finally caught up with her recently (2011) as she is still as busy as ever, even in retirement! We chatted about her most famous recipe which was shown on the Bob Braun Show. The story goes that Colleen was doing the food segment on that show for a time and one of the sponsors was Jiffy© Corm Muffin mix. Colleen was given a recipe for spoonbread by a lady in Kentucky which could be easily be made with the Jiffy mix. Colleen made up the spoonbread and suddenly" out of the blue" Jiffy Corn Muffin Mix had the highest local sales ever!

I wasn't familiar with this recipe but have tried it out on the family after getting it from Colleen and they all gave it an A+. This is great with chicken, turkey, roast beef or anything you want to serve spoonbread with. I think it would make a great buffet item for a church supper too.

Kentucky Spoonbread

Colleen: *"We make lots of soup at our house but this recipe goes well with any soup or stew. This recipe was given to me when we lived in Florence, KY."*

Stir together in a 1½ quart baking dish sprayed with Pam:
2 eggs (slightly beaten)
1 stick of butter (melted)
1 box of Jiffy© Corn Muffin Mix
1 small can corn
(or ½ can corn – about 7 oz)
1 small can creamed corn
(or ½ can creamed corn – about 7 oz)
1 carton (16 oz) sour cream

Bake at 375° for 40-45 minutes, until the center is done.
It is great with ham, turkey, chicken or beef.

NOTE: I really enjoyed making this myself and the family just loved it. This is the easiest spoonbread recipe I think I have ever seen too!

Paul Dixon

THE MAYOR OF KNEESVILLE

What can anyone ever say about "Paul-Baby?" I was thinking about how loved this man was by his fans and a true legend in Cincinnati Broadcast history.

During the 1960's and 70's he was the funniest man on WLW-T. No competition on that station from anyone. So if you loved Paul you know that "Kneesville" was the front row of the studio audience where Paul went with his binoculars to check out the short skirts. There was a lot of laughter as he used a water squirt bottle on the ladies knees or hung a dangling earring from an exceptionally short skirt. It was Paul who heard crazy stories and daily gave an audience member "The Big Salami." It was Paul who created the infamous "Chicken Wedding" on television.

The Chicken Wedding began when someone had sent him a rubber chicken who was cast as 'the groom" and then another rubber chicken who came along became "the bride." For months the viewers kept this whole event going

sending in clothing for the chickens personalities. Paul and his staff got the idea to get many of the local live TV hosts involved in the wedding too. Bob Braun, Vivienne Della Chiesa, Colleen Sharp and Bonnie Lou were part of the "big day." Bruce Brownfield and his band played the event. It is still one of the most watched re-runs on WLW-T as they did think to put this show on tape and save it.

I loved Paul Dixon and like many others wrote for tickets to the show but never did get there. I was in the hospital on the day I was to go and sadly watched it all from a hospital bed! Paul's staff heard the story and sent me a small room heater, which years later although it likely doesn't work I still have in my basement.

Paul died unexpectedly of a heart attack a short time later in 1974. Always he will be missed. I have no recipe from him except one for happiness. Start the day off with joy as he did, and perhaps a good cup of coffee. [CONTINUED]

I do not think that anyone ever kept track of how many cups of coffee Paul, Colleen Sharp, Bonnie Lou, Bruce, the Band and crew of the Paul Dixon show drank on a daily basis, but I would say several pots. On top of which they had coffee sponsors over the years who got plugs as the hosts chugged their hot steaming mugs of java during the show.

Commercials were all done live in those days and sponsors got the extra push of personal endorsements of their products. This proved to be an excellent tactic for the selling of products in the local markets. These are my tips for a great cup of coffee from a drip coffee maker.

PAUL DIXON'S

Tips for a Good Cup of Coffee

1. Use cold water fresh from the tap. Run the water and then fill the pot.

2. Select the best coffee you can afford. This may mean that you have to grind your own beans so consider buying a coffee grinder. You will not regret this.

3. To get the right balance of coffee and water there is "advice" given on many coffee packages and with the machines. A general rule is 1 Tblsp Coffee: 6 oz of water. (weaker: 8 oz).

4. Use unbleached coffee filters. Bleached ones are processed with chlorine and this can affect the taste.

5. Be sure to clean your coffee pot on a regular basis. The manufacturers usually will give you instructions. Most of these pots you can clean with ½ cup white vinegar and a pot full of water. Brew the vinegar and water and then run 2 pots of clear water through the coffee-maker, brewing the clear water to remove all the vinegar.

6. Be sure to either drink all the coffee when it is made or transfer into a thermal carafe. What happens if you leave it on "warm," is that it will continue to "cook" and really loses it's flavor. Making smaller amounts can also solve this problem.

Bonnie Lou

CINCINNATI'S ROCKABILLY QUEEN

I have always loved Bonnie Lou. She is so sweet. The only time I met her was in Shillito's some years back and she called me "honey" just like she called Colleen, Bob and all the other WLW-TV stars. Bonnie Lou was remarkable in that era of television being on the first regional country/western weekly television show: *The Midwestern Hayride*, appearing on the 50/50 Club and being a daily performer on *The Paul Dixon Show*. Bonnie Lou was not only her adorable self but a terrific musical talent making records, many personal appearances and live singing engagements. In my mind as a kid growing up with *The Midwestern Hayride*, I loved the fact that she could yodel. That was really cool. Some of my family is from Switzerland and I can't yodel! Sometimes in the bathtub I would try and it would sound more like a wounded coyote than a real "Yodel!"

I actually went once to *The Midwestern Hayride* when I was a very, very young. My father's mother, Grandma Mary lived near Albion, Pa. and had come to Cincinnati for a surgery. After she had recovered her one "dream" was to visit The Hayride. So my mother wrote for tickets and

we got to go. My Grandmother was absolutely delighted. Bonnie Lou sang, Willie Thall was funny and they had all that country music right there in the studio- live. The performers wore colorful costumes which we could never begin to interpret on our black and white TV sets. It was a memorable evening!

Bonnie Lou is actually a member of the Rockabilly Hall of Fame and you will be impressed to check out her long famous bio online. She made many records including the song "Daddy-O" and the "Tennessee Wig Walk," these were on the charts!

Now putting together this cookbook, I asked for a few recipes and typical of the big hearted and generous Bonnie Lou she sent me a bunch. She loves to cook! I am sharing with you two of them which are really great and a bit different. The shrimp spread for those of you shrimp lovers and a wonderful sweet potato casserole (you can never have enough sweet potato recipes!) So from Bonnie Lou's kitchen to yodel-lay-dee-who–YOURS– some new recipes!

BONNIE LOU'S

Shrimp Spread

When the Hayride is at your house!

2 (5 oz) cans shrimp, drain and mash
1 stick soft butter (not margarine)
1 (8 oz) package of cream cheese
2 Tblsp mayonnaise
2 Tblsp lemon juice
6 shakes of garlic salt

Combine and mold. Serve with crackers.

BONNIE LOU'S

Sweet Potato Casserole

3 cup cooked & mashed sweet potatoes (a tall can will do)
½ cup sugar
½ stick butter, melted
¼ teasp salt
2 eggs, beaten
½ cup milk
½ teasp vanilla

Mix above ingredients and pour (spread) into casserole.

TOP WITH THE FOLLOWING:
1 cup brown sugar (packed)
⅓ cup flour
1 cup walnuts
⅓ stick butter, melted

Mix and sprinkle over potato mixture.
Bake at 350° for 35 minutes.

Kenny Price

FROM THE HAYRIDE TO HEE HAW

Of all the stars in this book Kenny Price was the most unlikely to "go national." At 6 feet tall and over 300 lbs, he was nicknamed "The Round Mound of Sound." A native of Boone County, Kentucky, he briefly studied at CCM in Cincinnati. Then he began an amazing career from *The Midwestern Hayride* to hit records to the most popular national country television program ever; *Hee Haw*. Kenny had 34 singles make the charts. Most famous was "Walking on New Grass" which made it to the top ten in 1966 as did "Happy Tracks" his next single. Kenny was a big hit as well with national audiences on *Hee Haw* where he was teamed with LuLu Roman. He left us in 1987, too young, at the age of 56!

Although I do not remember him well from *The Midwestern Hayride*, I do remember him on *Hee Haw* and his great bass voice in the Hee Haw Gospel Quartet which featured Grandpa Jones, Roy Clark and Buck Owens. He sang his music as well as appeared in sketches on that program.

Kenny's wife, Donna wrote many songs for him including "Let's Truck Together." In the 1980's Donna Price also became famous on the Nashville Network when she teamed with Kenny and they did a travel show where they did trips in an RV visiting various points of interest called *Wish You Were Here*.

Humming "Walking on New Grass" right now– it seems fitting to add a recipe from Donna (Price) Fancher and remember the mellow songs and the cheerful personality of our own Kenny Price.

"Happy Tracks" Honey Almonds

2 cup whole almonds
¼ cup honey
2 Tblsp butter
1 cup (raw sugar)

DIRECTIONS:

1. Spread Almonds in a shallow pan
2. Place in a cool oven. Roast 350° for 15-20 minutes.
3. Over medium heat, heat honey and butter on low. Simmer 2 minutes, stirring occasionally.
4. Add almonds, simmer and stir for 2 minutes.
5. Using a slotted spoon, transfer almonds to baking sheet lined with parchment paper, or sprayed with non-stick cooking spray.
6. Spread almonds in a single layer and cool slightly.
7. To coat, toss almonds with sugar in a food storage bag.

Recipe from: Donna (Price) Fancher

Ann Holiday

I can remember at my junior high school my home economics classes were generally way out of date – we were stitching aprons for goodness sakes! They got more interesting when we took our "field trip" to visit Ann Holiday at the Cincinnati Gas and Electric Co. on 4th St. downtown. Usually the only time I went to CG&E for anything was at Christmas when we "did" the Christmas displays downtown and of course the incredible train display which filled the lobby. Who could forget those great free cookies to munch on they always gave everyone? This was a highlight of the yearly Christmas trip.

"Ann Holiday" was not just one gal but a bevy of real home economists trained in giving authoritative advice on the new appliances, gas and electric cooking, kitchen planning, lighting and cooking in general. The "Anns" were pleasant and attractive ladies too. From 1951 through 1970 they ran the bustling "Holiday Center" which hosted all kinds of groups. Recipe cards were the staple handout of these events as well as food demonstrations. (I still have floating around here a card for Tomato Aspic – which I think I made one time – not being a real fan of aspic it has since gotten lost!) Anyway, we were really impressed by the following recipe for Onion Butter Bites. Our Ann Holiday told us they were great for parties and I remember to this day "a wonderful cocktail snack"... which really stayed with me being not old enough to drink. (Of course that went along with art class where people who didn't want to sculpt could make ash trays – which kids did often. Think what would happen today!) This is a fun little recipe still and a reminder of days gone by. Direct from Ann Holiday to you!

Onion Butter Bites

Great for parties and as a cocktail snack!

½ package of onion soup mix
10 buttermilk biscuits, unbaked
½ cup (1 stick) butter or margarine

DIRECTIONS:

1. Stir the onion soup powder before dividing it to mix all the seasonings.
2. Melt the butter, then mix the soup to make a sauce.
3. Cut each biscuit into 4 pieces with kitchen shears. Place the biscuit bits in a greased 5 by 9 baking dish.
4. Cover with the sauce.
5. Bake at 450° 10-12 minutes or until golden. Makes 40 bits.

THE *Ronald Reagan Highway*

As long as I could remember, people were always talking about a highway to connect the eastside of Hamilton County with the westside. There were plans in the works my entire life.

This project was initially called the Cross County Highway (State Route 126) and was partially built from the East and from the West for a number of years. The midsection which ran through Finneytown, North College Hill and across I-75 not being completed for years and years. This project caused a lot of disruption too as, for example, Ed's Aunt Margaret lived in the path of this highway and so she had to sell her home due to the Cross County road project. She eventually ended up with her kids, Patty and Larry over on the westside.

Speaking of this eastside-westside business. It is a critical issue here in Cincinnati. You either live EAST or WEST of Vine Street which is the dividing point. Now this may not sound critical but it is in Cincinnati. There are definite differences between east and west siders. You don't really know this until you are in a Cincinnati "mixed" marriage. This is when (God forbid) an east sider marries a west sider. This is what happened when I married Ed.

OR the Cross County Highway to us locals –

I was a bonefide east sider and he was a dyed in the wool west sider! The conflict came with where to live to resolve this problem. It is difficult to just move to the other side of town on general principles.

The answer came when we decided to move to the north side–outside of Cincinnati to New Burlington, Hamilton, Co. just north of the city for our first married residence. For 30 plus years of marriage we have lived north of town which I believe has had a positive effect on our relationship. We have resided in Fairfield, Loveland and Lebanon all north of town! Other people have resolved this by moving to Northern Kentucky or even Southeastern Indiana.

...As for the Reagan Highway – it was dedicated after the Reagan years, in 1997, by his daughter Maureen. President Reagan was from Illinois and later California. In fact I don't think he ever even drove on this highway. However, I did run across a recipe for his favorite macaroni and cheese– so in honor of both east and west siders and for all the trouble the Reagan Highway caused, here is a bit of mac and cheese to be enjoyed by all!

Macaroni & Cheese

President Reagan's favorite recipe.

½ lb macaroni
1 teasp butter
1 egg, beaten
1 teasp salt
1 teasp dry mustard
3 cup grated cheese, sharp
1 cup milk
1 Tblsp hot water

DIRECTIONS:

1. Boil macaroni until tender and drain thoroughly.
2. Stir in butter and egg.
3. Mix mustard and salt with 1 Tblsp hot water and add milk.
4. Add cheese, leaving enough to sprinkle on top.
5. Pour into buttered casserole, add milk mixture, sprinkle with cheese.
6. Bake at 350° for about 45 minutes or until custard is set and top is crusty.

From undated/untitled newspaper clipping

Eat Your
Macaroni
& Cheese
"IT IS YOUR DUTY"

Shillito's

Once the first book, *Cincinnati & Soup,* hit the local shelves suddenly from out of nowhere came two other recipes from that great department store. Who could not just love Shillito's? I had a long relationship with the store on many levels. As a shopper, teen model, a Suzi Snowflake and then for a time I was an account manager and regional promotional rep. for Diane Von Furstenburg Co. I was constantly IN Shillito's and eating in the tearoom or first floor "grill" at the downtown store on 7th St. It was a great place too. Large departments of quality goods and then there was Shillito's basement which was the place for real bargains and the only "no frills" area of the store – excepting the offices and "backstage" areas of the store. At one corner of the first floor there was a marvelous bakery, candy and gourmet shop next to one of the exits on 7th St. This was a great place to pick up something to munch on the way home as the Shillito Garage was just across the street kitty corner to the department store. Most people I know who remember the 1960's and 70's have some memory of buying something, eating in the tearoom or just shopping at Shillito's.

Usually most people from that generation too remember Christmas at Shillito's which was a major event. It was always amazing that around Halloween every year during the 1960's , 70's and early 80's, a part of the toy department became transformed with incredible sets and mechanics into

Santa's Northpole Workshop. There were mechanical elves making toys, mailing packages, making candy, playing in the snow and then there was the "nerve center" showing the routes Santa and his sleigh would take. It was just amazing. At the conclusion of all of this was Santa himself and he was there in person to listen patiently to your wishes and take a photo. Everyone brought kids to this and there were some adults who just stood in the long, long line to just see the elves too. It was one of those things you just never got tired of. If you remember me mentioning my Aunt Marno in the last book – she had to find kids to GO and DO this and look reasonable in the process so she recruited Heather and Heather's mom (as she was Heather's godmother – a good move in this case!)

To start this story off you have to know that my Aunt Marno was an Olympic Shopper. By that, I mean that she would go to four or more stores and compare prices before she bought most of the time. This practice came to a screeching halt when she hit middle age and it got to be too much to do the important price comparisons. Then she tended to buy everything from Shillito's or Pogue's and forgot about this. Christmas shopping was also like this but in this case it was "SEE" everything Christmas in town. Now in those years, that was a genuine feat and also hard on YOUR feet!

Aunt Marno's Christmas Plan

Think about this itinerary:

» Park in the Shillito Garage.

» See The Northpole Exhibit in Shillito's (skip Santa).

» Go to the Arcade in the Carew Tower: See the Tree

» Go to Pogue's: See The Talking Reindeer, Pogie and Patter

» Go to McAlpin's for lunch at the Tearoom

» Go to the Provident Bank:
See their indoor Holiday Village, eat a free candy cane

» Go to the Cincinnati Gas and Electric Co:
See the train exhibit, eat a free cookie

» Return via Elder Beerman, See Santa.

» Head back to the Shillito Garage.

This was "the plan."

I doubt generals in the field ever have a plan like this one!! Anyway, all was well excepting one tiny detail. In 1980 we had a few unusually warm days in early December when this outing was to take place. The little trio set off to DO the itinerary with Christmas sweaters and coats on. As the day wore on it got unseasonably warmer and warmer to near 70 degrees! They all started to "melt" in the heat. Coats were carried along by mid-afternoon and it seemed more like midsummer than 4 weeks before Christmas! Even Santa Claus suffered during that short warm spell. Everyone did survive and wishes were told to the jolly fat elf himself and of course were granted later on but indelible forever was the tale of the summertime/wintertime Christmas march through downtown Cincinnati with Aunt Marno.

SHILLITO'S

Chicken Pot Pie

Served in the tearoom, this recipe was published in the Cincinnati Enquirer and is from an undated clipping from that paper as in the past it is yellowed from being "passed around" many times!

1/8 cup frozen peas
1/4 cup sliced frozen carrots
6 cooked pearl onions
3 oz or 1/2 cup diced cooked chicken (1/2 to 3/4 inch chunks)
3/4 cup sauce (recipe below)
1-2 oz. pastry to cover pie.

1. Cook frozen peas and carrots. Drain.
2. Place chicken chunks into small casserole and add vegetables.
3. Pour sauce over and bake at 350° until sauce bubbles.
4. Serve with pastry top over casserole dish. Makes one pie.

POT PIE SAUCE

3 Tblsp margarine
1 cup chicken stock
1 1/2 Tblsp flour
Dash pepper

1. Melt margarine, add flour and mix well.
2. Add stock, cook and stir until creamy. Add pepper.

SHILLITO'S *Cheesecake*

Served in the Tearoom and sold in the Shillito Bakery (The Shillito Kitchens also prepared food shown on the 50-50 Club and Bob Braun Shows)

CRUST:

18 single graham crackers, crushed
1 Tblsp granulated sugar
3 Tblsp melted butter

FILLING:

1 cup granulated sugar
24 oz cream cheese
5 eggs
1 ½ teasp vanilla extract
1 Tblsp fresh lemon juice

TOPPING:

1 pint sour cream
½ cup granulated sugar
1 ½ teasp vanilla extract

1. Mix the crust ingredients, pressing them into a 10" springform pan.
2. Mix together the sugar and cheese using a mixer. Add the eggs one at a time.
3. Add the vanilla and lemon juice.
4. Bake in preheated oven at 300° from 1 – 1 hr 10 min. Bake until set and top is puffed.
5. Mix together topping ingredients.
6. Remove cake from oven and spread topping on.
7. Return cake to oven for another 10-15 minutes.
8. Cool and then chill in the refrigerator.

Go Bearcats!

GO UNIVERSITY OF CINCINNATI!

Everybody sing: "University of Cincinnati, Bearcat Radio, W-F-I-B" OK enough of that... just this morning the jingle carts were racing through my head – "Audio 8- W-F-I-B.." eek there I go again – and now everyone who lived in the University of Cincinnati (UC) dorms are singing along too.

WFIB was the local station for the University of Cincinnati with a tower atop the Physics building and wired to the dorms. Everyone on campus got their news and "social info" from this station. IT was the communications central of UC.

I was in and out of UC several times and knew well several of the station managers. There was Dean...which was clever – that was his REAL name and when he made calls to advertisers they though he WAS a REAL dean which really helped get sponsors onboard...then there was and lastly Bear. Also there were some station engineers of note. For years it was George Smith and then in the late 1970's Ed Brinkman... hmmm I know that name. But my strongest connection with the station was my air shift which created quite a stir as I was the first woman on the campus to have a regular air shift. This was a real fight, each quarter I did the air shift as women's

"lib" was a pretty new thing and many of the weren't the least bit friendly about this. Exceptions were Thom, Ed (not my husband), John, Roger and Karl. Karl was nice because his air shift followed mine and also tended to be on "the outside loop" around there as well.

Now if you went to U.C. you know for certain that the Broadcasting Dept. was located in CCM . You had places in CCM where everyone went to hangout i.e. the "Scrounge Lounge" which was originally named by a gal named Janet when it was NEW.. so you can imagine what it deteriorated into by the time I got to grad school! Then too everyone got their fill of grease over at Mc Donald's in Tangemann Center so I will not be sharing their recipes.

What got me through college over there was hoagies. Meatball Hoagies. You could get them at a number of places near campus, Papa Dino's, Zino's and if you had any connections on the westside – from La Rosa's. I think between cold pizza, tuna hoagies, Cincinnati chili, cheese coneys and meatball hoagiesI did survive U.C. with a B.S. and an M.A. Go Bearcats!

Cheri's Meatball Hoagy

UNIVERSITY OF CINCINNATI SURVIVAL FOOD

2 hoagy rolls
12 frozen meatballs (cook according to the package)
1 small can tomato sauce, or an Italian sauce
if you have any around.
4 pieces mozzarella cheese
½ teasp Italian spices
*OPTIONAL: thinly sliced onions

DIRECTIONS:

1. Slice hoagy rolls
2. Heat tomato sauce and Italian spices to boiling on stove or in microwave.
3. Put cooked meatballs on ½ of roll. (6 per sandwich)
4. Top with sauce and then top with cheese.
5. Broil (or microwave) until cheese gets soft.
6. Put the top on and enjoy.

*If you like you can serve with the sliced onions.

This makes two hoagies – it is nice to not eat alone!

Cincinnati Food Favorites

Darcidoll, The Real Me!

Most people aren't their email address but one thing for sure is that I possibly am ! Way back in the 1970's in Cincinnati the Kenner Toy Company had their headquarters and design studios. There were really "cool" people who designed the "Star Wars" toys and the " Easy Bake Ovens." My neighbor Linda's husband was a sculptor who was fortunate enough to be employed at Kenner.™ Now this wasn't too important except he was running around sketching babies – like Heather (mentioned in *Cincinnati & Soup*) and having interesting guests such as the artists who were making a new fashion doll. One of these artists, Harvey, spent an inordinate amount of time in Arnold's Restaurant in downtown Cincinnati one night doing sketches by the ton on cocktail napkins of me while consuming copius amounts of alcohol and talking about his great danes in California. In addition, at the same time, I was just about everywhere in Cincinnati as a model in newspapers, T.V. and department stores. Talking to people who worked at Kenner in those days, it was a really creative atmosphere and people were encouraged to bring in all sorts of media and materials for the projects as well as local models.

In the case of the doll this wasn't done. Instead a series of photos and sketches were used to create the new product. Time passed. Over a year later *ta da* – I am in the Toy Dept at Shillito's downtown buying a gift when I come face to face with myself in a box! I went into denial over this, totally! The doll, needless to say, was only produced for around three years before becoming "collectible" and generally forgotten. Spin forward to the 1990's and my daughter Allison and I are in a bookstore and I find a book that has the doll in it – her first remark was, "You know Mom, that doll looks just like you!" – no prompting given. So what can you say? I have talked to artists who argue over this in both directions. I get emails from all over the place and have met a lot of collectors. I wrote a not very interesting book about this which was never published. Who knows? Who cares?

Darcidoll's Party Foods

IF I were a teenage fashion doll, I would have a party every day and wear disco clothes and sleep in a posterbed...right...

Here are some real party foods I like and serve:

RECIPES FOUND IN CINCINNATI & SOUP

Cincinnati Sliders
Cincinnati Hamburger Pizza
Shillito BBQ

Bourbon Wieners: see page 85

Meatballs:

1 package frozen meatballs:
Cook according to directions, then place in one of the sauces below and serve with toothpicks

SAUCES (HEAT):

1 cup Hickory Smoked Style BBQ Sauce OR
1 cup Italian Traditional Spaghetti Sauce OR
1 cup Sweet and Sour Sauce (Chinese style)

Dips:

1-16 oz carton sour cream
Add ONE (only) of the following:
½ cup crumbled bleu cheese OR
½ pkg dried onion soup mix OR
½ pkg taco seasoning mix (tex mex dip)
The above are really great with chips and crudités (cold veggies)

Tex Mex Chili Cheese Dip

This is the best hot four-season party dip ever. I got this years and years ago from my friend, Linda, who got it from her sister Nancy's boyfriend, Clint. The original name being "Clint's Dip" – Clint is long gone but the dip lives on. Where it originated I am clueless. Try this you will love it!

2 lbs process cheese loaf

PRE-COOK:
2 lbs of ground chuck
1 large onion
4 oz evaporated milk
1 (16 oz) jar salsa or taco sauce (mild or hot)
1 can refried beans

Put all of this in a crock pot and cook 2 hours before serving. Serve over tortilla chips.
Makes mucho!

Real Guacomole

SOMETHING GOOD FROM CALIFORNIA

While attending Monterey Peninsula College, I picked up this recipe clipped from an undated 1970's Los Angeles Times for guacamole. This is the very BEST guacamole I have ever made or eaten and I highly advise you try this one. You will love it! Think of the sunset over the Pacific Ocean and the crashing waves of Big Surf as you dip your chips into it...

1 soft avocado
2 teasp lemon or lime juice
¼ teasp cayenne or skinned jalapeno chile pepper (minced)
use the jalapenos sparingly unless you want it really hot
1 clove garlic, minced
1 small tomato, peeled and diced

1. Peel avocado and remove the seed.
2. Mash the avocado with lemon or lime juice. Guacamole is not usually perfectly smooth but still keeps a few lumps.
3. Add cayenne or chile, garlic and tomato. Mix well.
4. Serve at once.

Great with chips, on salads or Mexican dishes.
Makes about 2 cups.

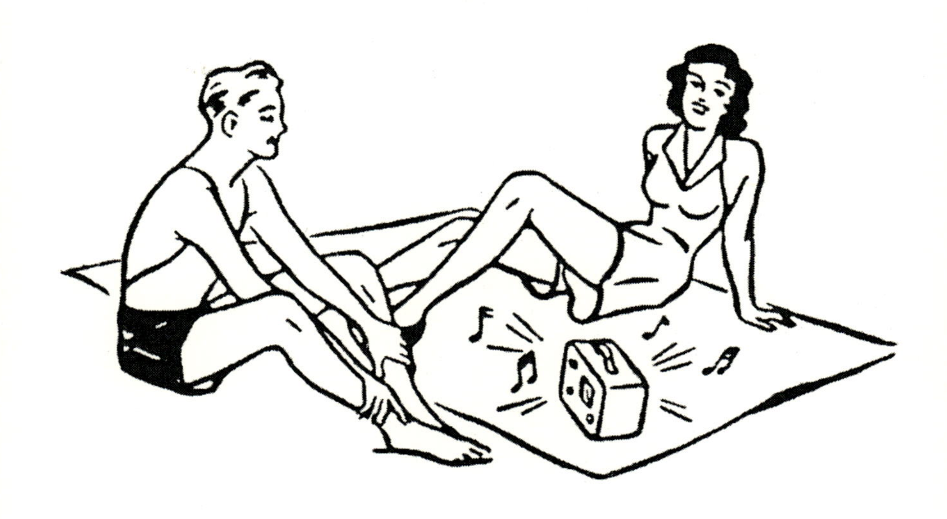

Think California, Ohio!

Sausage & "Kraut"

Which brings me to a really funny story which has nothing really to DO with sausage except maybe in a parallel universe –

My Aunt Marno was a woman ahead of her time. She was a true "career woman' in the 1950's, which wasn't done. She was a linguist and spoke and translated German, Italian and French. (She was my French tutor while I was in school. When I was attempting to express myself in France I blessed her name many times!) Aunt Marno also was the Treasurer and financial wiz for the Beck Studios, a stage equipment business. (She was unique, as a woman doing that job at that time as well as keeping all the books in French, which was also some sort of feat considering Carl, their accountant, did not SPEAK French!)

Aunt Marno had many interests in addition to languages. These included attending classical music performances, the Cincinnati Opera Guild (she was a life member and made

me one too) and the Cincinnati Art Museum where she took an evening class in "life" drawing. This was not just ANY drawing class, but the drawing of live models wrapped in towels or less. This is where the story gets interesting.

Every day the Studio got many parcels and a large number of deliveries. One of the delivery drivers was particularly muscular and handsome. Aunt Marno kept track of things like that. Models were always finding other jobs elsewhere and posing in the cold drafty Art Academy was certainly no treat! So time and again a new "model call" would go out. My Aunt in her enthusiastic desire to help decided to ask the delivery driver if he would want to model for the art class! I understand the driver declined, we are left to wonder what he thought of Aunt Marno's propostition. I will always remember her as a tireless patron of the arts.

A CINCINNATI HOME FOOD

Sausage & "Kraut"

1 lb sausage: this can be 4 Hamilton Metts or 4 Bratwursts or 1lb Smoked Sausage or 1lb Kielbasa
1 lb sauerkraut, fresh packed or canned
1-2 apples (peeled and sliced thin)
1 cup chicken stock
1 Tblsp vegetable oil

DIRECTIONS:

1. Gently prick sausages and then brown in a medium skillet in vegetable oil.
2. Add apples and cook about 4 minutes.
3. Drain some of the water off of the sauerkraut and add the kraut to the pan.
4. Add the stock.
5. Bring to a boil, then cover and simmer about 20 minutes.

Serve with mashed potatoes, rye bread and brown mustard.

YOU CAN LEARN TO
BE AN
ARTIST
Start DRAWING
At Home in Your
SPARE TIME!

Cincinnati Fish Story

THE ONE THAT GOT AWAY.....

This isn't about fishing off the Serpentine Wall or fishing in the Ohio or nearby lakes... but it IS sort of a fish story. It DOES include a gourmet "fish' recipe from Chef David King at the former Terrace Garden Restaurant from an undated and unmarked newspaper clipping. I also have another undated and unmarked newspaper clipping about Uncle Chris whose antics from time to time actually made the newspaper. So first from the old clipping an Uncle Chris fishing story:

CHRIS CHRISTENSEN, the peerless orchestra leader, annually goes fishing a way fur piece up in Canada with Merrel Ludlow, vice president of Beck Studios. The other day while eating in the Sinton Jet Chef, he was fiddling around with a large three-gang pike bait, preparatory to his expedition in July. He wanted to test the lure's action in water so he was dangling it around in a glass of water. The restaurant grew quieter and quieter as more and more diners noticed the unusual performance.

Suddenly a funster shattered the calm. "Hey Chris," he hollered, "they're biting better down at the B & G!"

TERRACE GARDEN SPECIALTY

Shrimp Scampi

This is one of several recipes which Chef David King shared with one of our local papers. The yellowed clipping has this great version of the dish and reminds one of the great food at the former Terrace Garden restaurant.

6 large fresh shrimp
2 cloves garlic
1 oz olive oil
1 oz butter
seasoned flour *(flour mixed with dry Italian spices)*
3 eggs, well beaten
½ cup milk
1 lemon
2 oz sauterne wine

DIRECTIONS:

1. Peel and devein shrimp, leaving the tails on.
2. Peel and crush garlic.
3. Combine egg and milk nix thoroughly.
4. In skillet, heat oil, butter and garlic.
5. Dredge shrimp in flour. Dip in egg mixture and flour again.
6. Saute until golden brown on both sides.
7. Squeeze juice from ½ lemon, then add sauterne.

Serve on a warm plate.

From undated/unidentified newspaper clipping

Graeter's Bakery & Ice Cream

A true Cincinnati tradition even to this day. I have fond memories of going to the local Graeter's in Pleasant Ridge for Nectar Sodas- still my favorite, or to the bakery in Western Hills with my Aunt to buy birthday cakes. My mother baked crooked birthday cakes but Aunt Marno always bought confectionary marvels from Graeter's. There was a reason for this.

Aunt Marno threw theme parties. I would like to share with you a story about one of these parties which was retold many times. It seems that one of her friends was having a summer birthday during Summer Opera season. They decided to meet before the evening's opera early over at the Palm Court Restaurant at the Netherland Hilton Hotel downtown for a celebratory dinner. My Aunt and Uncle Chris (her husband, the big band leader) bought another wonderful cake from the Graeter Bakery and then on top of the cake built an accurate stage set for the evening's opera "Boris Godunov." They copied the set from a photo and even dressed a tiny doll as Boris. (These really super table decorations were done

for everyone so birthdays were not just marked – they were EVENTS!) The friends gathered for cocktails and dinner with no one noticing a very plain looking man in the corner of the restaurant who was observing them and the attention the opera set was getting from not only the party but the "wait' staff and other patrons entering the restaurant. The gentleman came over to the table to check all of this out and it turned out to be Norman Triegle, the singer who was heading over to Music Hall to PERFORM the role of Boris!! He delightedly pointed a finger at the little set and doll saying "That's me!" Everyone was totally charmed by him and there was a flurry of handshaking and autographs signed. This was a party to remember.

Double Butter Coffee Cake Clone

To this day the fabulous Graeter's bakery has never let out the secret of their cakes however a few years back there was a Double Butter Coffee Cake recipe which started showing up at a lot of church socials. This is NOT the real Graeter Coffee Cake but it has a lot of the rich flavor which we have come to expect from their products. This recipe has been passed around a bunch. I heard it was even published in a newspaper once? It seems to "fit the bill" for the richness of the "real" Graeter's coffee cakes. This is one you will love! (Especially you out of towners who pine for the "real thing!")

CRUST:
¼ cup sugar
¼ cup shortening
¼ teasp salt
1 egg
1 pkg active dry yeast
½ cup warm milk
2½ cups flour
1 teasp vanilla

FILLING:
2½ cups sugar
1 cup butter or margarine
dash of salt
2 eggs
¼ cup light corn syrup
2½ cup flour
¼ cup milk
1 Tblsp vanilla
1 teasp almond extract
1 teasp ground nutmeg

Undated/unidentified newspaper clipping

A CINCINNATI DELIGHT

CRUST:

1. Cream together sugar, salt and shortening
2. Add egg.
3. Dissolve yeast in the warm milk.
4. Add flour and vanilla to sugar mixture blending thoroughly.
5. Knead on a floured board 10 minutes.
6. Place in a lightly greased bowl. Cover and let rise in a warm place for 1 hour or until it has doubled.

FILLING:

While you are waiting for the crust to rise:

1. Cream sugar, butter and salt.
2. Add eggs and syrup.
3. Add the flour alternating with milk, nutmeg, vanilla, almond ex. and nutmeg, blending well.

CAKE:

1. Divide dough into 2 parts. (This recipe makes 2 cakes)
2. Gently pat each half into a 9" x 9" pan. Press dough about halfway up sides of pan. (This will hold the filling)
3. Prick holes in the dough.
4. Pour filling over the crust dough and let stand about 20-30 minutes.
5. Bake at 375° for 30 minutes – be careful NOT to over bake!
6. Let cool. When cool dust the top with confectioners sugar and additional nutmeg.

Cincinnati Roast Beef

There is always a holiday roast going on in many Cincinnati homes just as families always gather for dinner in our town. This brings me to the "flying roast" story of an Easter long long ago.

When I was a kid, our family divided the holidays yearly up amongst my mother's sisters. My mother hosted Thanksgiving and Christmas, her younger sister, Becky (short for Ethelwyn) had the Memorial Day picnic. (This was due to the fact the one year she had attempted to cook a frozen turkey and it took 5 hours of waiting to eat it so they never gave her another shot at it – some things are NEVER forgotten)

Aunt Marno and Uncle Chris usually had Easter (and Fourth of July) at their apartment or house and always had either a Roast Beef or Pork Roast. They had a charming apartment at one time in Walnut Hills overlooking the Ohio River. That year a wonderful dinner was planned, baked potatoes, fresh green beans and green salad along with the roast beef. The apartment was decorated in lovely shades of beige with a new modern coffee table from Closson's in the shape of an artist's palette. Perched on three legs it was artistically

balanced but not very stable. My Uncle Chris was going to use it this time for a "holding table" for food while a folding table was set up next to the dining table. He carefully placed the large and steaming roast beef on the coffee table. At the same moment, on the other side of the table, my younger brother, Alan, made the wrong decision to lean on the table thus launching the roast airborne. Needless to say it plopped down on the beige carpet and juice flew everywhere. Never missing a beat, Uncle Chris grabbed the meat fork and retrieved the roast off the carpet with one stab. With aplomb he carried the roast into the kitchen and proceeded to wash off the large piece of meat. My Aunts, mother and the rest of the group were on their hands and knees with towels and cold water attempting to save the rug and furniture which forever after had a "meaty" tinge to them. The washed roast was returned to the dining table and consumed. In retrospect, I can only say at that moment I was relieved that they did not have a dog or there would have been another scene where we would have had to wrest the meat from a pair of canine jaws!

Roast Beef

In the old days you could order a roast beef from the butcher shop and that is still the best way to get your holiday roasts. Even with the advent of many of our super super super stores there is nothing like the old fashioned butcher shop meats which are sadly going the way of the dinosaurs. I still like to be able to chat with the person cutting my meat and lately more of the "big markets" are keeping their meat counters and butchers due to the requests of customers for more personal service and higher quality meats.

Oven Roasted Beef is really easy to prepare and I would certainly try the recipe below.

MEAT:

Buy a true "oven roast," Rolled rump roast,
Sirloin Tip Roast, Eye of the Round Roast.

SERVINGS:

Think about ½ lb per person (minimum) you will want leftovers so think bigger than the actual table servings.

A GREAT FAMILY DINNER

ROASTING:

1. Take raw beef roast out of the refrigerator about 20 min. before cooking. You can pre-heat the oven to 450° while you are waiting. (DO NOT USE A FROZEN ROAST!)
2. Rinse and pat dry roast beef and put on a rack in a roasting pan. Season the top with one of the following:
   a. salt, pepper and garlic powder OR
   b. Montreal Seasoning OR
   c. other dry seasoning of your choice.
3. Immediately turn the oven heat down to 325° and put the roast in the oven with a meat thermometer in the thickest part. Cooked roast beef should have an internal temperature of: 130-135° for rare, 140-145° medium and 150-155° for well done.
4. Most beef roasts will go about 20 min. per pound for rare and 30 min. per pound for well done if you are trying to calculate this in "time". Sometimes they take a bit longer depending on the thickness of the roast etc. It is always best to check the above temperatures on your meat thermometer to make the decision if the roast is done or not.

Always check too with the butcher for advice. Beef Tenderloin roasts can cook in as little as 30 minutes and they too are "oven roasts!"

Gone But Not Forgotten

More great recipes from our favorite restaurants which are now but a memory....

As I started writing the first book suddenly I heard from a lot of folks with more old recipe cards, as well as clippings from old newspapers and lots of great stories from their families too. I am going to share a few of these treasured dishes with you .

Grammer's Restaurant

HIGH DUTCH VS LOW DUTCH-SAUERKRAUT BALLS

This recipe came from the old Grammer's Restaurant on Liberty Street in Over the Rhine. It opened in 1871 and has gone from a restaurant to a bar and I understand that recently it will re-open again as a restaurant. For years it was one of the centers of THE German culinary experience in our city. This was one of the places when Ed and I were first married that we made a stop at regularly for dinner as we both love really great German food. This recipe card is really old so I don't know who got the recipe or where but it is still a favorite and one that makes any time of year "Oktoberfest!"

One of the interesting things about Cincinnati is the German influence in the region. You have Over The Rhine where many Cincinnati families have their German roots and in Covington the Mainstrasse . There was at one time a lot of German spoken in this city . There were many German street names and on a lot of the older churches in town there are still to be seen German inscriptions. In the hopes of being more patriotic during World War 1 many German names also passed out of existence. German was a second language for children and in many schools in those old days as well.

There was in the past a variety of distinct German dialects spoken here. Where Cincinnatians came from during the mid 1800's was the deciding factor. Those who spoke what was commonly called "High Dutch," were Germans from Southern Germany and Switzerland; "Middle Dutch," German from Central Germany; or "Low Dutch," German from Northern Germany near the Netherlands and Alsace/Lorraine. This caused a lot of problems for students as the main dialects spoken in southwestern Ohio were Low and Middle Dutch and the one being taught in schools was "High Dutch." My Mother and Aunt Marno, for example, got no help from my grandmother who was fluent in Low Dutch when they were growing up and had to wing it at school. My Aunt became fluent in the language, mother gave up. This was one reason I was not raised speaking German. Of course at the time I grew up French was considered THE "international" language and rather than learn a dialect of some type it seemed best to just go with the flow.

GRAMMER'S RESTAURANT

Sauerkraut Balls

1 lb mashed potatoes: Cook and mix with 1 teasp butter and a little milk and salt and pepper.
1 ½ lbs sauerkraut, wrung out
4 oz finely chopped ham
1 Tblsp parsley
2 Tblsp chopped scallions
1 Tblsp mustard
flour/egg wash and fresh bread crumbs

DIRECTIONS:

1. Combine all ingredients except flour, egg wash and crumbs.
2. Mix well and shape into 1" diameter balls.
3. Bread with flour then the egg wash. (egg wash is made with a beaten egg with a little milk)
4. Roll in the fresh bread crumbs.
5. Deep fry or pan fry until golden brown. Drain on paper towels.

Serve with mustard or cocktail sauce.
Makes several dozen.

GOOD TO EAT
LUNCHES & SANDWICHES
QUICK
SERVICE

Shuller's Wigwam

WHERE EVERYONE IN COLLEGE HILL USED TO MEET

My mother's family lived in College Hill. It seemed that everyone IN College Hill sooner or later ended up dining at the Wigwam. I can remember having a wedding anniversary dinner there when we were first married. The food was really great and reasonable and there was a "better restaurant" feel about the place with white tablecloths and attentive servers. Many people I know had their wedding receptions at the Wigwam or large parties there for that reason. For the regular diner at the Wigwam a favorite order was the famous hot slaw. Again this recipe was published and passed around a lot to get to me. Hmmmm with all that travel it still tastes amazing today. Here from the long ago past...Hot Slaw.

SHULLER'S WIGWAM

Hot Slaw

This recipe from Leo Shuller, a former owner.

ham fat (fat cut off of a ham)
vinegar (cider)
EQUAL AMOUNTS OF:
sugar
cabbage, shredded for cole slaw

DIRECTIONS:

1. Cut ham fat into cubes ¾" to 1" each.
2. Cook in skillet until browned and slightly crisp.
3. Drain off grease and reserve browned ham.
4. Heat vinegar and sugar in amounts to suit taste
5. Portion shredded cabbage into salad bowls.
6. Ladle 1½ oz hot vinegar + sugar mixture over cabbage.
7. Then ladle 1½ oz crisp ham fat over cabbage.

From undated/unidentified newspaper clipping

Terrace Garden

A FAVORITE DOWNTOWN GATHERING SPOT

The Terrace Plaza Hotel, later the Terrace Hilton Hotel was in 1948 the most modern hotel in downtown Cincinnati. With no windows for 8 floors you shot up on the elevator to the 8th floor lobby where you also found the Terrace Garden. This was a unique restaurant which was outdoors on a "terrace" during the summer in the very old days and a skating rink during the winter. Now that was the original plan but I remember mostly eating indoors at the Terrace Garden as they gave up the outdoor deck after a while due to the heat and cold. Also in the same building upstairs was the famous Skyline Dining room and the even more famous the bowl shaped glass paneled Gourmet Room. These two restaurants were some of the most unique and expensive in Cincinnati at the time. [CONTINUED]

I remember having eaten in the Gourmet Room one time with of all people, pianist, Lorin Hollander and in the Terrace Garden numerous times over the years. The great thing about the Terrace Garden was you could just run in there and have a quiet lunch above the traffic and noise of the city while being right in the hub at 6th and Vine! I do remember one time meeting my Aunt there and seeing Steve Allen in the elevator. (He was in town for a book signing but unfortunately at that moment I did not have a copy of the book!) It was one of those places where the "elite met to eat."

Recently while doing more research for this book, I ran across in my archives an undated clipping with several recipes from the Terrace Garden's attributed to Chef David King; the Shrimp Scampi, and the Chicken Breast Parmigiano for Two. Both of these recipes are so wonderful that I decided to include both in the book. Now from a glamorous restaurant from the past, gone but certainly not forgotten...Chicken Breast Parmigiano.

TERRACE GARDEN

Chicken Parmigiano for Two

2 (6-8 oz) boneless breast of chicken
4 oz parmesan cheese
2 oz chopped, fresh parsley
flour (seasoned)
8 oz tomato sauce
2 servings pasta
2 oz butter
2 oz olive oil
3 eggs, well mixed
½ cup milk

1. Warm tomato sauce and set it aside.
2. Skin Chicken breasts and cut them in half. (Today you can get skinless chicken breasts which is what I use in this recipe) Pound them until flat and thin.
3. Mix eggs & milk, pour into a shallow pan such as a pie pan.
4. Mix the parsley and cheese, put it in another shallow pan.
5. Dredge the pounded chicken in flour, then dip in egg mix.
6. Press chicken into cheese and parsley and coat well.
7. Start pasta cooking.
8. Combine butter and oil in a large skillet and heat.
9. Saute coated chicken breasts until golden brown and both sides cooked through.
10. Drain pasta well and mix with enough tomato sauce to color.
11. Place pasta on platter and top with ½ of remaining sauce.
12. Place sautéed chicken breasts on pasta and cover with remaining sauce.

JUST ACROSS THE ROEBLING BRIDGE

Northern Kentucky

As *Cincinnati & Soup: Recipes from the Queen City and Great Soup* upon publication immediately crossed the bridge into Kentucky, it seems fitting to include some great recipes from Northern Kentucky in this encore book.

I promised all my friends in Kentucky, this includes: Mary, Jim, Sister Barbara, Venus, Ryan and a bunch more, that I would do something special for our neighbors in the Bluegrass state. After all they are just across the bridge from us and have wonderful food there too!

Newport

Calm today but the Memories of Yesteryear Linger on...

When I started to write my Kentucky chapter, I was trying to think of where to start when it dawned on me that I first needed to be in glamorous old Newport with it's honky tonk ways. I thought about writing about Ed's grandfather who used to live on the south end of the Covington, Mainstrasse and often walked to the Anchor Grill for his meals and it is the home of 24/7 goetta. I was dating Ed and had dinner there one evening. Maybe that is what won Ed over to marry me?

To get back to the "neater" story- Allison and I went on the Newport "Gangster" Tour recently and trotted around the cleaned up Newport, Kentucky. Once loaded with strip joints on every corner, gambling and mobsters it WAS "Las Vegas" before Las Vegas at least according to our tour guides. It is pretty calm now with most of the local "spice" being contained in the Dixie Chili Parlor or the lonesome "Brass Ass" lounge which is one of the few "nightspots" from the "old days" still around. [CONTINUED]

As the "Gangster" guide told his stories I did recall Uncle Chris playing in Newport in it's "hay day." As a musician he had bands and ensembles which from time to time played the big clubs owned by Glenn Schmidt, including the Rendezvous. Usually things went ok and these were just "gigs." However there was often a serious big time big money poker game in the back room and sometimes things did get "rough" which meant getting out of there before all heck broke lose. One night things got way out of hand and he and the small band which he had playing there barely got out with their instruments before havoc ensued. They also had trouble getting paid as well which pretty much ended Uncle Chris' work with the Schmidt clubs even on a "fill-in" basis. Newport was one of the "hot spots." I was too young to go under any circumstances at that time!

Bourbon Wieners

Never served in Newport Night Spots –
but found at many a Kentucky Party!

1 (16 oz) package of cocktail wieners
[*I prefer smoked sausage ones but choose what you like the best, in the old days you just cut up wieners and used those, these are much neater*
1 cup ketchup
¼ teasp mustard
½ cup brown sugar
NOTE: May substitute 3 Tblsp currant or strawberry jelly
¾ cup bourbon

DIRECTIONS:

1. Mix everything but the wieners together and heat.
2. Pre-cook wieners in the microwave about 2 minutes.
3. Add to sauce and simmer 10 minutes.
4. Serve in a mini-crockpot or chafing dish with toothpicks.

THE *Beverly Hills Supper Club*

You can't mention entertainment of the legitimate sort without mentioning the wonderful Beverly Hills Supper Club. Everyone from the generation before me really has the memories there, but I have mine too. My first trip there was when I was five. I was really well behaved at five – I might add.

My mother was in the hospital birthing my brother and I was staying with my Great Aunt Martha, Great Uncle Vernon, Cousin Lee and her husband Chick out in New Burlington, Hamilton Co., Ohio. Someone got tickets/a table or had an "occasion" and decided we should ALL go to Beverly Hills. They could not after all leave a 5 year old to their own devices which was reasonable thinking. So we all went to dinner at Beverly Hills in the "Showroom" and saw Lena Horne. Yep now there was something to talk about at kindergarten. She was absolutely amazing with a great voice and extremely beautiful . I think I was not supposed to tell anyone about this but it was such a great experience - everyone including my parents heard about this ad naseum.

Beverly Hills is gone forever but in the haze of the distant past many special nights and font memories remind us of what was once "America's Showplace."

Bourbon Steak

GRILL THE BEST - DUMP THE REST!

Although this bourbon steak was not served at Beverly Hills it is elegant enough to be served at the best barb-b-ques and "grill outs" around. It may be served with gourmet vegetables and salads or packed off to a tailgate party for your favorite team. One thing for sure is that everyone loves this recipe featuring Kentucky Bourbon and you will always get many requests for this great steak recipe.

1-2 lbs steak to marinate

MARINADE:

1 teasp granulated sugar
¼ cup Kentucky bourbon (nothing else will do here!)
2 teasp soy sauce (or worchestershire sauce if you do not have soy sauce)
2 Tblsp water
½ teasp garlic powder
½ teasp ground black pepper

1. Mix all of ingredients.
2. Add the steak and put in a covered dish or zip top baggie for at least 4 hours.
3. Grill.

NOTE: Some fans of this dish have told me that they always "test" the bourbon before making the marinade which consists of a hearty shot. These folks are always extremely happy grillers I might add!

Covington

I have never lived in Kentucky but I am a good culinary visitor and love the food of our Ohio River neighbors. After college, when Allison moved to Northern Kentucky, she had her first residence in the historic district of old Covington. Later she moved to Ft. Thomas. There are so many great communities in the area and famous recipes that people have done whole books to them! I have two Covington recipes as Covington and Newport ARE the big centers of Northern Kentucky. Many restaurants are in the area and many have a featured dish, the Hot Brown Sandwich. The original is from Louisville and was in legend and tale, served at the Brown Hotel there. There are many variations of how this is prepared. This is the one we like.

THE *Kentucky Hot Brown*

Use individual baking dishes for each serving – as this goes into the broiler

IN EACH DISH:

1 piece bread with the crusts trimmed off
1 slice cooked turkey breast
2 slices tomato
2 slices of cooked ham or 2 slices of bacon
Top with: Cheese Sauce*
Top with: Parmesan Cheese: Sprinkled on top of each sandwich.
Broil until lightly browned on top.
Serve immediately

*CHEESE SAUCE: You can make any type of a cheddar cheese sauce or a quick one using processed cheese loaf.

DIRECTIONS:

1. Cube up 1 cup of processed cheese loaf in a microwave bowl, add ¼ teasp dry mustard, 3 Tblsp milk. Mix.
2. Microwave about 1 minute- or until cheese looks softened.
3. Remove and stir until it is smooth.
   Pour over the sandwiches.

Covington: The Mainstrasse

Ed's family spent a lot of time in Covington. The Brinkmanns (in those days they had an extra "n") lived all over town. At one point they had a store and saloon near old 11th St. and Greenup Sts. near what is now the Cathedral Basilica of Covington. Interestingly they were right at the heart of where the Covington School of artists lived and met. Frank Duveneck was a regular at their place as he lived just a few doors away. When I first met Ed I got to meet his aged grandfather who actually remembered as a child of 3 or 4 years meeting Duveneck. What impressed Ed's grandfather was some cheese crumbs being caught in his huge and bushy moustache. There was a lot of serious art talent in Covington in those days. Now art is coming back during the new renaissance of the area and perhaps as I am writing today there is another Duveneck lurking just outside the art world's radar – getting ready to burst "on the scene" shortly.

In honor of the Covington School and in honor of the "free lunch" counters which were so popular in saloons of the time, I would like to include my recipes for pickled beets and pickled eggs which were standards of the time at any free lunch counter around 1900. They are still good today and great for summer dinners, picnics and buffets.

Pickled Beets

2 cans beets (sliced- do not use the whole ones)
½ cup granulated sugar
½ cup white vinegar
[*In the old days they also used cider vinegar – they used what they had*
10 all spice
1 small onion sliced thin
*hardboiled eggs

DIRECTIONS:
1. Drain the beets.
2. Put the beets in a glass jar (which has a lid) with the sliced onions on top.
3. Heat together the vinegar and the sugar until the sugar dissolves. Nearly boiling. Add the allspice.
4. Pour over the beets.
5. Let slightly cool.
6. Put lid on and put in the refrigerator for 24 hours.
7. Serve the next day.

Pickled Eggs

6 hardboiled eggs
½ beet juice *(this was what you drained off of the beets you are pickling in part one)*
1 cup vinegar (cider or white)
1 cup granulated sugar
1 small onion sliced thin
10 all spice

DIRECTIONS:

1. Peel eggs.
2. Mix and heat the beet juice, vinegar and sugar. Add the all spice. Dissolve the sugar.
3. Put in a glass jar (with a lid), add the onions on top.
4. Pour the vinegar, sugar, all spice, beet juice liquid over the eggs.
5. Cool and close the lid.
6. Chill in the refrigerator for 24 hours before serving.

A Second Helping of Soup

MORE SOUP TO ENJOY

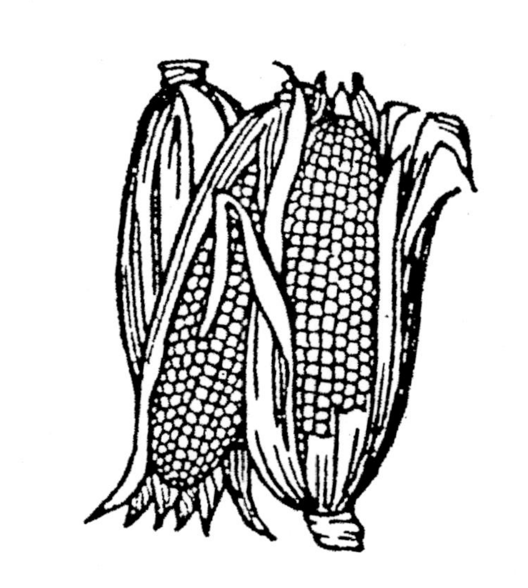

Popcorn makes a great crouton and is fun for the kids!

Popcorn Soup

If you think that this is a recipe using popcorn as a main ingredient you are definitely mistaken – it is the extra added croutons on the top of this delicious soup!

Popcorn Soup started as a Thanksgiving tradition at our house when Allison was around five years old. I had read some really "cute" suggestion to get kids to enjoy new soups by using popcorn in lieu of the regular bread croutons .We tried it just one time on corn chowder and it has not stopped since.

I will remember the first year we did it as it was a crazy Thanksgiving to say the least. 1987. Yep that was it. I decided to have Thanksgiving in my country kitchen over in Loveland. I had everyone. My parents, my in-laws, my sister, April (who was unmarried and still sitting at the "children's table"), my brother Alan and his wife, my Aunt Marno and then us. Now this was a gang of individualists. My Aunt Marno did not eat turkey so for her there was a "ham" dish, my sister April is a vegetarian so for her "vegetarian stuffed cabbage rolls" and then there was the turkey with all the trimmings. This was an amazing amount of food. People like my Dad, who was an "omni-vore" and ate everything, had a really full plate.

We also did cocktails and snacks before dinner. By snacks I mean simple things like chip and dip. (Ranch dip as a lot of folks did not like french onion!) Something to go well with the famous bloody marys I made for family events. This is the way to true family harmony. Two of them and your [CONTINUED]

could eat dinner with Attila the Hun and still be civil! Anyway, I did this fabulous dinner virtually singlehanded. All was well until about halfway through the meal our rescued apricot toy poodle Ollie went missing. As it turned out Ollie was having a great time on his own. He had crept back into the family room where the chip and dip had been left and had his little face in the dip bowl . A cute little face dripping with ranch dip! Now unless you have ever seen a toy poodle with a face ful of ranch dip you haven't lived..and then there were the digestive after affects which really made the day after Thanksgiving memorable. Thanksgiving has been a lot quieter since then. We have since learned that no matter how trustworthy a dog seems, they can make the most awful "food errors."

Popcorn soup is something your kids will love and I suggest that unless you want it to BE a tradition at your house serve it some time, other than Thanksgiving.

The recipe for this corn chowder comes from my good friend Catherine's Aunt Blanche. This is the soup Catherine makes when she is knee deep in corn out at her farm every summer. To get that great "farm flavor" I would also suggest fresh corn or "freezer corn" which is corn you buy in the summer, cut off the cobs and pop into the freezer. It is nice to be able to pull out some fresh corn after the first frost. Even with canned or regular supermarket frozen corn this recipe is a dandy one especially with the "popcorn" floating on the top.

Corn Chowder
WITH POPCORN CROUTONS

2 slices of bacon
1 large onion, chopped
1 cup celery, chopped
1 green pepper, seeded and diced
2 cup potatoes, diced
1 can corn kernels (*2 cups fresh corn kernels)
1 can cream corn
2 cups milk
salt, black pepper, Worcestershire sauce to taste

Simmer until the vegetables are tender, about 45 minutes.

POPCORN CROUTONS:
Place about ¼ cup unpopped popcorn
in a brown paper lunch bag.
Microwave about 1-2 min. or until corn stops popping.
Top soup with the popcorn when serving.

Ein, Zwei, Drei —

It used to be that anywhere you looked in old Cincinnati or "Zinzinnati" (as the local Germans pronounced it) there was something to DO with Beer- spelled "bier" in the old days. At one time there were many breweries in the Queen City which sad to say most are all gone. Some of the trade names have been recently "resurrected" by other brewing companies looking to peak local sales. Sad to say but these are lost recipes too! I have the funniest beer story though I must share with you.

My mother was a graduate of a secretarial "college." She had her very first job offer from old Bruckmann Brewery. She was very excited about getting a job but as a non- drinker of alcoholic beverages this was going to be something to deal with. Her friends were of no help in this nor her father who told her that "the drinking fountains at Bruckmann's were plumbed into the brewery and that instead of water in the fountains – there was beer!" It took months before my mother would drink out of the water fountains there. Eventually she did find out that they were giving her a bad time and did take a chance at the water fountains. I'm sure most of the employees wished for beer in the fountains but it never was to be!

Beer Cheese Soup is made in many German heritage areas of the US. It is not distinctively a "Cincinnati" specialty but does reflect our brewery heritage and is another of the unusual soup recipes which I have enjoyed putting in my books.

A TART TREAT FOR BEER LOVERS

Beer Cheese Soup

4 Tblsp margarine
½ cup diced onions
½ cup diced celery
2 cups diced raw potatoes
12 oz lager beer
2 cup chicken stock
½ teasp dry mustard
2 cup cubed process cheese loaf
1 cup grated cheddar cheese
dash of hot sauce

DIRECTIONS:

1. In a soup pot, sauté the onions and celery in the margarine.
2. Add chicken stock, beer , potatoes, and dry mustard.
3. Bring to a boil and then simmer for about 20-30 minutes until potatoes are tender.
4. Add cheeses , dry mustard and hot sauce. Stir until cheese is melted.
5. Serve with crusty bread and of course another beer to wash it all down.

A Delicatessen Favorite

For as long as I can remember whenever Ed and I have eaten in Cincinnati delis he is always looking for a bowl of Sweet and Sour Cabbage soup. We have debated as well over the years the various recipes for this dish. It is another of those recipes which is made from leftover beef originally but now can be made fairly quickly and easily with prepackaged beef stock. This is great on those cold and rainy days when you really want a tasty bowl of soup to ward off the chill.

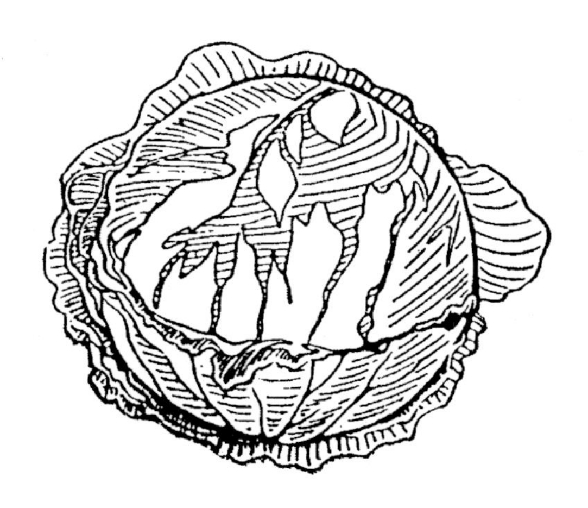

Sweet & Sour Cabbage Soup

4 cup shredded cabbage
1 stalk of celery, chopped
½ medium onion, chopped
½ cup carrots, chopped
1 Tblsp margarine
15 oz can diced tomatoes
32 oz beef broth

TO TASTE :

3½ Tblsp concentrated lemon juice
3 Tblsp brown sugar
(Start with these measures and if you like your soup sweeter or more tart, go from there)
garlic powder (also to taste)
1 cup water: *again depending on how strong you want your soup add water.*

1. Saute celery, onions and carrots until wilted in the margarine.
2. Add broth, 4 cups of shredded cabbage and tomatoes.
3. Bring to a boil and add garlic powder, lemon juice and brown sugar.
4. Simmer on a low boil for about 1 ½ hours or until cabbage is tender.
5. IF you feel the soup is too strong add water or adjust spices and reheat before serving.

SERVES ABOUT 4

From Eastside Mall Lunches

The first time I ever ate Baked Potato Soup was with my Aunt Marno over at Funky's Blackstone Grille in the Kenwood Mall years and years ago. We would go in there and consume huge quantities of it. The restaurant is long gone but in memory is their terrific soup. At one time the recipe was published in the paper but with several home moves THAT clipped recipe has somehow disappeared. So here for all you lovers of GREAT homemade baked potato soup is my version of it put together from memory. I think it is a reasonable "clone"in fact I ate it yesterday for lunch and yes you can eat it on the westside, the northside and the southside too.

Shopping was always fun with my Aunt as she was the original "Olympic" shopper. As noted from the Christmas "pilgrimage" around town she was good for the "long haul." Most of you Cincinnati "bargain hunters" know about this already. The Malls were shopping palaces as there were big anchor stores and lots of small stores to check out.

I especially have a story for those of you who will be shopping for others in the shopping centers and malls. Get yourself a present too. This comes from a Christmas shop long long ago involving a troop of people including Uncle

Chris and that other baby Heather. I am not sure where to begin but Uncle Chris was running around looking at everything and Heather decided (at the age of one) that she did not LIKE Santa Claus and had an immediate fit, so we had a screaming baby along, much to her mother's dismay and in the Northgate Mall which was packed with shoppers.

In the midst of Pogue's I was looking at winter hats and gloves when suddenly my Aunt said to me, "Try on the red velour hat". It was really cute. I tried it on and then gasped at the price tag. It was after all Pogue's and Pogue's was more expensive than a lot of the other stores. It was during a recession as well and I was a student working limited hours so the cute little red hat was out of the question. My Uncle had since wandered back and although he at the time was also on "part-time" hours said, "We'll take it." It was a little like being Mimi in "La Boheme" and getting a hat for Christmas. I had it for years and years and always enjoyed wearing the little red hat in the winter months. Remember that when the holidays come YOU are special too so DO treat yourself with something good – even if it is only a flavored coffee or a bite of chocolate – YOU deserve it!

Baked Potato Soup

1 (15½ oz) can chicken broth
½ cup milk
½ teasp minced dried onions
½ -¾ cup instant potato flakes

TOPPINGS FOR SOUP:
¼ cup chopped fresh onions or chives
¼ cup sour cream
1 baked potato (chopped with skin on)
2 Tblsp chopped crisp bacon or salad real bacon bits
¼ cup shredded cheddar cheese

1. Mix together chicken broth, milk and dried onions. Heat through.
2. Add instant potato flakes. Use enough to thicken soup. Stir and heat until soup begins to boil.
3. Remove from heat and put into 2 bowls.
4. Top each bowl with ½ the amount of fresh onions or chives, chopped baked potato, sour cream, bacon, and cheddar cheese.

This makes about two servings and is a quick easy lunch or is great on a cold winter day.

SERVED ON THE EASTSIDE
BUT LOVED ALL OVER

Bravo! Encore!

CINCINNATI CLASSICS –
TOO GOOD NOT TO REPEAT

Music Hall

Music Hall has been the scene of many great events in the history of Cincinnati and thankfully it will continue on with continuing renovation in the works. IT has been the home of the Cincinnati Symphony, Cincinnati Pops, the Cincinnati Opera and of the Cincinnati May Festival to name the "big players." There have been many other events there too – over the years. During my parents generation, Music Hall was the scene of many high school graduations and local concert events. During my generation, Music Hall became the home of the Cincinnati (Summer) Opera which prior to that had been held at an outdoor pavilion out at the Cincinnati Zoo. As a kid that was where my Aunt Marno took me to the opera out at the zoo. Sometimes it was too hot, it rained buckets, there were warnings for tornados and they still finished the opera. But it did have it's fun moments. Peacocks calling during the soprano arias, seals barking during tenor arias and noise from traffic in the distance. It was such fun, that I lied during junior high school so that I could get to usher and see the performances free. I was taking voice lessons and figured it would help me learn things not covered by my teacher at the time the elderly Norma Richter. Norma was a diva and had played the Summer Opera and also the old San Carlo Opera Co. (with Ed Molitore another friend of my Aunt's and was a really great old gal. She and "Ed" M. [CONTINUED] were really inspirations at that time. These WERE opera singers of the first class. IF nothing else I got a good start in singing and learned a great deal about poise which has always done wonders in any social situation. Sometime later when I was in high school, I met Jim and Thom (two friends from up in Dayton) at a Music Hall event who thought I was "very sophisticated" at the time due to my "poise."

I can't let Music Hall go without at mention of a former and almost forgotten conductor, the late Thomas Schippers. I just loved Thomas Schippers. Tom. He was a great musician and an interesting human being. One summer, I seriously injured an ankle and sitting around, my Aunt (who had already committed to this group) suggested that I consider auditioning for a pick-up chorus being put together for *The Damnation of Faust* for an opening concert of the Cincinnati Symphony. As a student I was really excited about this opportunity, however when I got there, I hobbled in to find that all the soprano slots had been filled and all they had was a second alto and some tenor spots open so I jumped at the opportunity to take any spot. My Uncle agreed to be in this as well – and it was the only time we all sang or actually performed together in anything. So off to rehearsals we went. Performances arrived and there was Tom Schippers seeing him from the front was pretty cool. He was just charming to everyone from little me

hobbling around to the famous Metropolitan Opera singers singing the leads. One performance he was so wound up in the score that he forgot to "cue" the chorus to sit after they sang. This wasn't a problem for anyone but me and my crutches. During the intermission Schippers made a point of apologizing to me for this mistake and hoped I did not suffer any pain due to his error! As I said he was adorable.

He also did an incredible amount of smoking when not on the podium which as it turned out later led him to any early demise. It was an amazing performance. I did forget to mention the attractive young school teacher from Portsmouth, Ohio, who stood in the gallery to sing the role of the Celestial Voice- Ms. Kathleen Battle. Ms. Battle was so nice and such a positive person and had that incredible voice which would make her world famous in only a few years. I could not mention Music Hall without this story.

Cincinnati Chili

As those of you who own book 1 know, I am big on keeping our local recipes. My first book featured a Cincinnati Chili from the 1940's – using a spice bag and all the older style seasonings. I went through another stack of old newspaper clippings to find this one which is obviously later. I think one of the issues I have with it is that the allspice is left IN the chili which if you have dental work can be a potential land mine. Anyway- here is another version of the old standard. You be the judge and watch out for those allspice!

1 qrt water
2 medium onions, grated fine
2 cans (8 oz) each tomato sauce
5 whole allspice
½ teasp red pepper
1 teasp ground cumin seed
2 lbs ground beef
4 cloves garlic
4 Tblsp chili powder
2 Tblsp vinegar
1 large bay leaf
5 whole cloves
2 teasp Worcestershire sauce
½ oz bitter chocolate
1 ½ teasp salt
1 teasp cinnamon

ANOTHER RECIPE

DIRECTIONS:

1. Add ground beef to water in 4 qrt.pot.
2. Stir until beef separates into a fine texture.
3. Boil slowly for 30 minutes.
4. Add all other ingredients. Stir to blend.
5. Bring to a boil, reduce heat and simmer uncovered about 3 hours.
6. For the last hour the pot may be covered after the desired consistency is reached.
7. Refrigerate chili overnight so that fat can be lifted off the top before reheating and serving.

SERVE: Alone (1 way)

WITH: Spaghetti (2 way)
Spaghetti & Cheese (3 way)
Spaghetti, Cheese & Onions (4 way)
Spaghetti, Cheese, Onions & Red Beans (5 way)

Goetta

Yes, this was in my first book. There is no getting around a GREAT recipe. There are people who are frantically searching for a quick goetta recipe – especially folks who live out of town! So here it is again and some of the story. Goetta began in the stockyards. Thrifty German Cincinnatians could get pork bones for nearly "free" in the early days. The bones were boiled around 10 hours and mixed with onions and pinhead (steel cut) oats to create the original goetta.

No more long hours over the hot stove we now have Modern "Quick" Goetta!

SERVE GOETTA:

1. Fry up in a pan and serve on toast with an "over easy" egg on top.
2. Serve as a "side" at breakfast with eggs and toast. May be topped with maple syrup.
3. Recipes for this include: pizza topping, burrito filling etc.

Modern "Quick" Goetta

1 roll sage sausage
1 cup pinhead or steelcut oats
1 cup onions or 3 teasp dehydrated onions
½ teasp salt
1 teasp dried red pepper flakes
1 teasp ground black pepper
water

ON THE STOVE:

1. In a large pot put 3 cups of water. Break the sausage into small bits and add to the water along with the onions. Cook for about 10 minutes over a medium heat.

IN MICROWAVE:

2. Mix 2 cups of water with 1 cup of oatmeal and ½ teasp. salt. Microwave 3 minutes. Then stir. Do this 3 times (9-12 minutes total)
3. Drain the sausage and onion (this removes a lot of the grease and fat from the goetta)
4. Add the oatmeal and sausage to the pan. Add the peppers and mix.
5. Put in loaf pans and chill.
6. When thoroughly chilled, slice and fry or slice and freeze for later use.

NOTE: This goetta is more dry than commercial goetta and will crumble more due to the lower fat in the finished product.

The Happy Ending

Every story must come to a happy ending in my world and here is another easy dessert for you to enjoy and entertain with. I would also add another Uncle Chris story as well to chuckle on.

I can only imagine this one. Back in the 1950's and 60's upwardly mobile people did a lot of entertaining over at The Maisonette Restaurant in downtown Cincinnati. It was elegant, 4 stars, french chefs and really great cuisine. All the rich and the famous ate there as well as 99% of the business community. It was a truly unique and amazing dining experience. This brings me to Uncle Chris. As an orchestra leader he had an incredible sense of humor and was constantly"on" which was often an interesting situation.

One evening he was early to meet some people for dinner outside of the Maisonette and as it was a fairly nice evening he was outdoors. As people left their limos and cabs he just stood there and started greeting them. "Welcome to the Maisonette..." and so on. Now this was before stores started the greeter position which is common today – so this really raised a few eyebrows to be greeted at this very exclusive restaurant.

Uncle Chris' party did arrive to find him doing this and got another good laugh. What can you say? Maybe in retrospect the Maisonette did need a greeter or they might still be here today? After all, it is great to feel welcome.

Black Forest Express Cake

I designed this dessert for people who are in a hurry who just love chocolate and cherries. It is just amazing. I have served this at birthday parties and even took it to Chris and Belinda's Christmas gathering where people swarmed in and consumed the cake in under 10 minutes (that set the all time consumption rates for the cake!) I hope that you too will enjoy this...it is irresistible.

1 small iced chocolate cake
[*This can be a thawed frozen one or store bakery one. I prefer the frozen ones*
1 can cherry pie filling
1 jar chocolate "Jimmies" (decorative chocolate sprinkles)
1 can whipped cream
*OPTIONAL vanilla ice cream

1. Put cake on decorative or serving plate.
2. Sprinkle and with a knife put the sprinkles into the icing on the sides of the cake.
3. Drain off some of the pie filling from the can as there is usually more filling than cherries.
4. Pour over cake.
5. Cut and serve topped with whipped cream. *Vanilla ice cream is also good with this.*

Your Local Recipe Finds ~

FROM THE KITCHEN OF:

INGREDIENTS:

DIRECTIONS:

Your Local Recipe Finds ~

FROM THE KITCHEN OF:

INGREDIENTS:

DIRECTIONS:

A BIG THANK YOU

There is no way to DO a book like this without mentioning some of the people who have helped in creating the book in some way. To my late Aunt Marno Beck Christensen and Uncle Chris (Grant) Christensen for their contributions to my life and who without their zaniness there would not have been these books! April, Alan, Heather and Aunt Becky for their invaluable contributions that have kept me laughing. Merrel and Jean Ludlow and Carl Kohrman for their additional story ideas. Catherine Estill and her Aunt Blanche, for the new corn chowder recipe, Linda Kovach and Nancy Buscher for the chili cheese dip. Thanks also to Mrs. Margaret Thomas, Mr. and Mrs. Tom (Patty) Riehle, Mr. and Mrs. Larry (Jennifer) Thomas, Dr. Dick and Ruth Jameson, Elaine & Jeff Parker, Becky Brinkman and all my wonderful friends and colleagues I have met along the way on this journey of food, fun and saving great memories and recipes from our past.

Special thanks to Erin Beckloff of iNkY WiNKe for her amazing covers and graphic design.

Also to the special people who were so great to add recipes and information:
Rob Braun, Wray Jean Braun, Colleen Sharp,
Bonnie Lou, and Donna (Price) Francher.

ABOUT THE AUTHOR

Cheri Brinkman has lived much of her life in Cincinnati and is an avid cook. She is the author of the much loved *Cincinnati & Soup: Recipes from the Queen City & Great Soup.*

She has enjoyed numerous career "adventures" including, fashion model, actress, singer as well as working in the broadcasting field with her most exciting adventure being a public speaker and writer.

Cheri is a graduate of Monterey Peninsula College and the University of Cincinnati. In recent years she has been a college educator with U.C., Miami and DeVry Universities teaching communications classes.

CONTACT: cincinnatandsoup@yahoo.com
FOLLOW: cincinnatiandsoup.blogspot.com